101 Ways to Improve the Game of Football

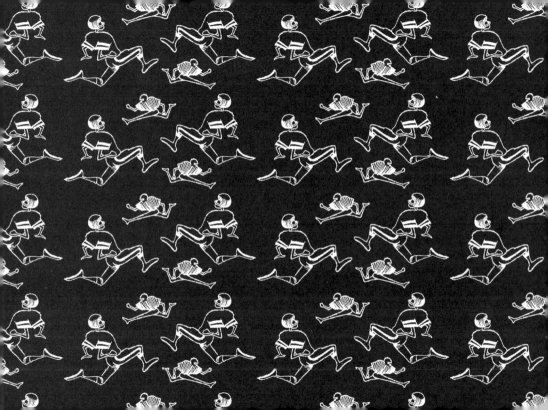

Published by Addax Publishing Group Inc.
Copyright © 1998 by Clay Latimer
Designed by Randy Breeden
Cover Design by Deborah Ramirez

For information address:
Addax Publishing Group, Inc.
8643 Hauser Drive, Suite 235, Lenexa, KS 66215

ISBN: 1-886110-57-3

Distributed to the trade by Andrews McMeel Publishing
4520 Main Street
Kansas City, MO 64111

1 3 5 7 9 10 8 6 4 2
Printed in the USA
Library of Congress Cataloging-in-Publication Data

Latimer , Clay 1952-
        It's 3rd & long, so— : 101 ways to improve the game of football /
by Clay Latimer.
        p. cm.
        ISBN 1-886110-57-3
        1. Football — United States — Humor. I. Title.
GV950.5.L38 1998
796.332'0973—dc21   98-27608
                                                                     CIP

101 Ways to Improve the Game of Football

by Clay Latimer

Illustrated by Brad Kirkland

ADDAX
PUBLISHING
G R O U P

DEDICATION

To Loraine and Monica

ACKNOWLEDGMENTS

Most books are collaborative efforts, and this one is no exception.

The list of thanks should start with my wife, Loraine, and several friends, including Ethan Rosen, who laughs at anything thrown his way.

I'd be remiss not to credit *Sports Illustrated* and it's on-going supply of wacky anecdotes and football oddities. I can't remember a time I didn't turn to *They Said It* as soon as I got my grimy hands on the latest issue.

Thanks to several other books, including *Football Hall of Shame 2* by Brush Nash and Allan Zullo, *Football Shorts* by Glenn Liebman, and *The Book of Truly Stupid Sports Quotes* by Jeff Parietti.

I'm especially indebted to the people at Addax Publishing, including Bob Snodgrass and Darcie Kidson, whose encouragement and professsional insights were once again invaluable.

INTRODUCTION

For many Americans, football has become an out-of-mind experience.

A Notre Dame fan threatens to sue because his new tattoo is misspelled "Fighing Irish."

To honor Buddy Ryan, her idol, a Kansas City woman slugs her fiancee at their engagement party.

A New York entrepreneur announces he's developed a mechanical hand to attach to your TV - so the lonely have someone to high-five, too.

Jeff (Deli) Dellenbach, a 300-pound NFL center, admits he's so big he can fit his wife and three kids inside his boxer shorts. And has.

Ex-Chicago Bears linebacker Bryan Cox proclaims he rose to his feet and screamed "My boy, my boy" when Mike Tyson bit off a chunk of Evander Holyfield's ear.

Football-wise, reality bites.

Too many coaches are a heartbeat away from a personal riot. Too many fans and journalists are lewd louts. Too many players are orbiting a planet no one else has been able to locate.

Not surprisingly, everyone keeps calling for improvements.

But no one ever answers the damn phone, not even the friggin' cellular.

Until now.

It's 3rd & Long, So ... provides 101 improvements that run the gamut from A-to-B, er, Z.

Let's begin the change-process with a pop quiz.

Which is more maddening?
A. Players with rings in their navels.
B. Coaches with air in their heads.
C. Owners with kited checks in their wallets.
D. Joe Theismann
E. None of the above

The answer is E, because A-thru-D don't even compare with $13 beers, noon-to-dusk games, self-enchanted losers, sore winners, liquor-gutted scribes, goofy stream-of-anxiousness broadcasters, wrung-out coaches ...

Not to mention a cast of heroes from your worst nightmares.

Oh, football retains much of its barbaric charm.

For example, Ex-Dallas Cowboys coach Barry Switzer set a goal of scoring 27 points per game before the gig was up for him. "If we get two touchdowns and three field goals, we've got our 27." Yo Barry: That's 23.

The Pittsburgh Steelers locker room has never been a hotbed

for scholarship, either.

"We're more aggressive, more mobile, more smarter," said Greg Lloyd on why the Pittsburgh Steelers had better linebackers than the Chicago Bears.

Players make more money than sense. Defensive tackle Sean Gilbert said "No" to the Washington Redskins' 3.6 million contract because a "revelation from God" told him he was worth $5 million.

Buffalo's 300-pound Glenn Parker has a guiding force as well: food. A few years ago, he and a high school buddy attempted to break the local record at an all-you-can-eat Rhode Island buffet table.

They scored a TKO victory.

"Steve had what we called a triple-double ...meaning he ate 21 lobsters, 12 filet mignons, and five dozen assorted cocktail shrimp and baked stuffed shrimp. I had 18 or 19 lobsters and 11 steaks. As we were dunking our lobster tails in our glasses filled with butter, they finally stopped serving us lobsters."

Coaches have tried to impose weight limits on players, not to mention sanity limits. But these are trying days for them as well. Everywhere they look, they're tabloid prey.

A North Carolina high school coach was slack-jawed when newspaper types actually criticized him for running up 100 points against an all-deaf team.

But football keeps rolling along, especially the NFL, because of the staying power of its bread-and-butter fan: the middle-aged male.

These guys are very unique, demographically speaking.

Beer remains the cornerstone of their diet. They still get a big kick out of knock-knock jokes. They remain, by and large, Elvis Men. And a good game still sends them higher than 15 kites.

But the bad games? They begin to resemble a country horse asleep on his feet. Or an Englishman.

"Don't you think three and one-half hours is rather much for a one-hour game?" asked one of our English cousins after watching the American Bowl in London.

Added another Great Briton: "I've never seen so much standing around. It makes cricket seem almost action-packed."

At least American fans have some artificial appreciation devices. For example, a Canadian company talks of producing a noise-maker that emits booing, cheering and even gun-fire.

Many fans don't need mechanical help; they need dire help.

Several stirred-up followers of the Chicago Bears removed a Packers fan from a bar, then duct-taped him to a stop sign under a placard that read 'Packers Fan.'

A San Diego Chargers fan bit off the ear of a Raiders fan. A woman in Denver rode through a downtown mall on a horse - buck naked (she, not the horse) - to win a couple free tickets.

College fans use well-honed career skills to get what they want.

A resourceful Texas A&M alumnus with a whole bunch of free time filed a request under the state's public information act to obtain a copy of the Texas playbook.

An Ohio State bulletin advertised the police report listing the drunk-and-disorderly conduct that led to the arrest and subsequent firing of Michigan coach Gary Moeller.

For die-hard fans, a Tennessee firm offers coffins in your school colors.

They might have to start burying mascots as well.

South Carolina's decked his counterpart from Jackson State

because he kept trespassing on the Gamecock's side of the field. The Hog - Arkansas' mascot - underwent knee surgery after an entanglement with his counterpart from Auburn.

Cheerleaders are as American as shopping malls. So what happens when a group of 'em from a South Carolina high school motor down to Florida for a regional competition. They get busted for shoplifting. Being competitors, they actually had an intra-squad contest to see who could grab the most loot.

Jerry Springer, call your office.

101 WAYS TO IMPROVE
THE GAME OF FOOTBALL

Modern football is comprised of four main elements: players, coaches, fans, the media. Some elements are intertwined. For example, Frank Gifford is with the media, but since he gushes ad naseum about the wonders of football, he qualifies as a fan and cheerleader as well. Steve Spurrier is a coach, of course, but his spiteful remarks about Florida's opponents are as witty as any columnist's.

"The real tragedy was that 15 hadn't been colored yet," Spurrier said to fans after 20 books had been destroyed by fire at Auburn's football dorm.

Ricky Watters is a player, but he's also a know-it-all of the fourth rank. So he counts as a coach and media member too.

We don't know where to put the Chicago Bears' Todd Sauerbrun.

To start with, a punter isn't really a football player. And he had a curious answer to a rather simple question. After returning from his honeymoon, he was asked where he was married.

"I don't remember," he said.

FUN WITH FRACTIONS

A survey of the nation (including parts of darkest Wyoming) was conducted to figure out what makes football people tick - or explode.

The results are rough estimates because only 2.3% bothered to return the survey, and 86% of the returned forms included (a) protracted religious pronouncements or (b) the questions were bizarrely misinterpreted.

A. FANS:

93% - Believe they could've played in the NFL if their high school coaches hadn't screwed 'em over or their high-school girlfriends hadn't gotten pregnant.

80% - Believe they could still make an NFL team if they had a couple months to get ready and their wives and bosses would just get off their backs for once.

43% - Wear baseball caps that advertise heavy-equipment dealers.

0.2 % - Watch PBS

87% - Would vote for John Madden for President

B. COACHES

98.5% - Believe Vince Lombardi was "this century's Abraham Lincoln."

72% - Believe they were a world-famous general in another life.

85% - Are worried their best player will appear on the TV show "Cops" with a digitally blurred face.

92% - View the 1950s as Eden.

93% - Believe a sportswriter's natural habitat is a cesspool.

C. THE PLAYERS

100% - of collegians hope to play in the NFL. Second career option: Courageous Hollywood action hero.

97% - Get a big kick out of jokes about bodily functions.

97% - Watch professional wrestling "religiously."

95% - Believe Ronald Reagan was "the best president in the country's history; might have been smart enough to be NFL Commissioner as well."

8% - Can name all the presidents since Reagan.

D. THE MEDIA

1% - Played football in either junior or senior high school.

2% - Played any sport in either junior or senior high school

2.5% - Spoke to a girl in either junior or senior high school.

97.5% - Spend a rare day off catching up with Rotisserie League chores.

100% - Become increasingly eccentric as the years pass.

83% - Are terminally flabby.

FOOTBALL: HELP IT BECOME ALL IT CAN BE 101 IMPROVEMENTS

NO. 1

No pain, no game.

This isn't cricket. Or baseball.

So enough of this anti-violence stuff. Boys will be boys. Take Chris Spielman, for example. When he was a little tike, his grandmother got down on her knees to give him a hug. Thinking she was ready for some football, Spielman ran up to Grandma and slammed his head into her head, knocking her on her back.

In his first organized football game, the nine-year-old Spielman broke a player's arm and nearly knocked another senseless. Parents immediately circulated a petition to ban him from the league.

Spielman rules!

NO. 2
Nike: Swish this.

NO. 3
Head cams

Watch enemies bump each other off - up close and bloody.

Head Cams

NO. 4

Require coaches to wear uniforms, like baseball managers.

NO. 5

The ground can't cause a fumble. Neither can the sky or wind.

NO. 6

No hand-holding in huddle. (Looks odd. Is odd.)

NO. 7

Be true to your school.

During sex*, ask partner to wear school's jersey. Or have the team mascot tattooed on your buttocks.

*It isn't asking that much. A survey at a Florida college measured the emotional and physiological responses of fans to erotic pictures and images of Florida college jock-stars.

The subjects were more turned on by local jocks than sex.

NO. 8
Penalty box

NO. 9
West Coast offense not allowed on East Coast.

NO. 8

NO. 10
Extend goal posts the width of playing field.

NO. 11
Offensive linemen must have less than 50% body fat.

NO. 12

Require team owners to eat stadium food.

The price of rancid $20 nachos would quickly drop to $19.

NO. 13

Politically correct nicknames not accepted.

NO. 12

NO. 14

Coaches who spread joy on their walk through life.

The morning after the Buffalo Bills 34-3 win over the New York Jets in 1989, assistant coach Nick Nicolau floored assistant coach Tom Bresnahan with an uppercut to the chin. Then he placed him in a headlock and ran him into a wall. The incident left a hole in the wall the size of Bresnahan's head.

NO. 15

Coaches shows must be accompanied by parental warning:
Prolonged viewing may induce acute drowsiness. Side affects:
Lowered pulse rate, acute depression.

NO. 16

Lifetime ban for any player caught doing a Full Monty during a game.

NO. 17

The Society to Prevent Buddy Ryan.

NO. 16

NO. 18

If the ball goes out of bounds, the play isn't over.

If the ball goes into the crowd, the play isn't over.

If the ball goes out of the stadium, the play isn't over.

NO. 18

NO. 19

Last-place NFL teams play in Rose Bowl.

NO. 20

Limit Joe Theismann to 500 words per quarter.

He's like one of those airport announcers: He never stops.
Don't ask Theismann to explain the theory of relatively, either.

"Not everyone can be a genius. Not everyone can be Norman
Einstein." – Joe Theismann

NO. 21

Players not allowed to dump Gatorade on coaches in inclement weather.

NO. 22

Players with gigantic bellies can't wear skin tight jerseys.

NO. 23

Mass substitution in mid-action, like hockey.

NO. 24

Owners' school.

Learn at the feet of such masters as Georgia Frontiere.

NO. 25

Convert to the metric system.

Pittsburgh Steelers fullback Jerome Bettis scored on a 9.144 meter run in the fourth quarter Sunday to conclude a 61-meter game-winning drive against the San Diego Chargers.

The 120-kilogram bruiser slipped through the grasp of 140-kilogram linebacker Junior Seau on the drive's first play.

Cool, huh?

NO. 26

Doo-rags in school colors.

NO. 27

Salary cap (includes cost and upkeep of luxury sedans) for Division I college teams.

NO. 28

Books that will sell the game:

1,001 Jokes from Barry Switzer

Hi-jinks Galore

Paul Tagliabue: "I've Got Game"

Mike Ditka: "My Love Poetry"

NO. 29

Every NFL team qualifies for playoffs - Fans are fossilizing in their seats, so give 'em something to lose it over.

NO. 30

Cut-rate Prozac for Raiderphiles - They're teetering on the brink.

NO. 31

Zero-tolerance policy for Lou Holtz - His BS is copious.

NO. 32

Sideline cages for kill-crazy linebackers. Why? Read on:

John Elway wasn't sure when he strolled to the line of scrimmage in his first NFL game. Pittsburgh Steelers linebacker Jack 'Fangs' Lambert was licking his bloody chops. "I was standing right across the line from him," Elway said. "He had no teeth and he was slobbering all over, and I'm thinking, 'You can have your money back - just get me out of here ... I can't even tell you how bad I wanted out of there."

No need to tell ex-San Francisco 49ers receiver Mike Shumann. He was completing a route during a game against the Steelers when all hell broke loose between Lambert and co-linebacker Jack Ham, who'd picked off the pass.

Lambert sprinted to Ham, then began violently shaking his own

NO. 32

teammate as well as spitting into his face.

A weird macho rite of celebration?

Hardly. Lambert was fuming because Ham had entered his "zone" to make a scene-stealing play.

"I was making about 25 grand at the time and I remember thinking, 'I can make more money bartending. Do I really want to play in this league with psychos.'"

NO. 33

Eliminate a quarter - Decrease boredom.

NO. 34

Eliminate a linebacker - Increase scoring.

NO. 35

Show Seinfeld re-runs on Diamond Vision for the benefit of slumberous fans.

('Cannonball Run' south of the Mason Dixon Line).

NO. 36

No more than 75 TV time-outs per game - fans are running out of profanities .

NO. 37

Save the Raider Nation

Fortune isn't smiling on Al Davis and his Oakland Raiders these days; it's crackin' up.

Save 'em by taking the following steps:

1. Crack down on drug and arms dealers at home games.

2. Establish a 10-day waiting period for purchase of season-tickets in order to weed-out psycho fans.

3. Ship Al Davis to World League.

NO. 38

Lower goal posts, allow defenses to have goalies.

Increases dramatic tension by forcing teams to forego mindless field goals.

NO. 39

Protect valuable young quarterbacks from themselves.

During a 1997 game, Washington Redskins quarterback Gus Frerotte scored a touchdown, spiked the ball, then sprinted 20 yards to head-butt a thick concrete wall.

Suffering from a jammed neck, he was rushed to a hospital and missed the final half and overtime of a game that ended in a 7-7 tie.

The monosyllables were flying in the Skins' locker room after that game, which might have cost the team a division title.

NO. 40

Unruly fans are subject to trades.

Especially the ones who aren't endowed with reason.

NO. 41

Drop Roman numerals from Super Bowl.

American kids can barely read, much less decipher these alien figures and the complex meanings behind them.

NO. 42

Empower mascots.

In 1976, the University of Florida's Wes Chandler raced to the winning TD in his team's come-from-behind win at Auburn. As he crossed the goal line, the War Eagle, Auburn's mascot, dive-bombed the stunned wide receiver. As Chandler desperately beat back the attacking bird, the official dropped the flag and assessed a 15-yard penalty against Auburn for "illegal participation by a mascot."

NO. 43

Build positive feelings by having all the fans hold hands and sing combaya after each game.

Also: Group hugs after big plays.

NO. 44

Bye month for the St. Louis Rams - They aren't big, but they're slow.

NO. 45

Designer uniforms, including jerseys by Armani and Gucci cleats.

It's not whether you win or lose, but how chic you look doing it.

NO. 46

Men who think on their feet.

"People say I can run through a brick wall. Why would you run through a brick wall?" Miami Dolphins fullback Larry Csonka.

NO. 45

NO. 47

Some Boogie Nights with the BrighamYoung Cougars.

NO. 48

Players who respect authority.

"If you want a messenger, call Western Union," Joe Don Looney
to the coach who asked him to run-in a play to the huddle.

NO. 49

Buy one franchise and get one free.

NO. 50

Competency tests for sportswriters and sportscasters.

"He's going off holding what looks to be a left leg," play-by-play man Phil Stone as an injured Texas AM player left the field.

During a game Curt Gowdy was broadcasting, a downpour left puddles on the field. "If there's a pileup out there, they'll have to give some of the players artificial insemination."

NO. 51

Quarantine Bryan Cox

During the first seven years of his career, Bryan Cox flipped off fans in Buffalo ($3,000 fine); flipped off and castigated a ref (fined $82,352, a week's pay); spit at fans in Buffalo ($7,500); fought a Buffalo running back ($10,000 fine); called the commissioner and his advisors "clowns"; challenged the Cincinnati Bengals bench to a fight, and threw his helmet against Green Bay.

He also broke a Northern American record by using 38 profanities during a five-minute, post-game tirade. Fans have run out of profanities to describe this kind of slapstick unreality.

NO. 52

A franchise for the human-animal kingdom of Los Angeles.

Don't let the third millennium begin in La-La-Land without gridders.

NO. 53

Help players get a life.

"If we didn't have a huddle, Jim would have no social life," said New York Giants quarterback Phil Simms about teammate Jim Burt.

During the 1963 training camp, New York Giants coach Allie Sherman saw a light on in one of the players' dorms. When he opened the door, he discovered a player he'd cut the week before watching TV.

"Hi coach," said punter Joseph Whelan. "Listen, this is great. I didn't have anything planned for the summer. I love the food. I've made a bunch of good friends. And now I don't even have to go to practice. This is a great summer vacation."

Alas, Whelan was sent home.

NO. 54

Moms, don't let your boys grow up to be Cheeseheads.

A nine-year-old recently stuck his head into the mouth of a 16-foot, 2,850-pound bronze jaguar's statue at Jacksonville's stadium. As his mother snapped a picture of him, he screamed, "I can't get my head out, Mom!" He was stuck for an hour before workers sawed off one of the cat's teeth.

Did the boy learn a lesson?

"Yes. Don't stick your head in a Jaguars mouth."

NO. 55

Mom, don't let your boys grow up to be gridders.

Cal-State Fullerton defensive lineman Ron McLean was so enamored with the game of football that he treated his uniform as an animate object. Every night, he'd gingerly put his equipment into bed and settle into bed next to it.

"I always pretended my gear was alive and that it was playing the game with me," he said. "Guys would ask me what my equipment was doing on the bed and I'd tell them it was resting up for the big game."

NO. 56

To avoid explosive post-game press conferences, which embarrass the sport, reporters should be extremely mindful of the losing coach's fragile psyche, especially with TV cameras present. A defeated coach doesn't have a short fuse. He doesn't have a fuse at all. A reporter shouldn't:

A - Interrupt him to correct his grammar.

B - Volunteer to list all his strategic errors.

C - State all the reasons a better coach would've won.

D - Suggest alternative employment.

NO. 57

Stop coaches from publicly mocking their own players.

Florida State coach Bobby Bowden on Reggie Herring: "He doesn't know the meaning of the word fear. In fact, I just saw his grades, and he doesn't know the meaning of a lot of words."

NO. 58

Men who care.

In 1971, the Oakland Raiders conducted two days of meetings before beginning formal practice. That made newcomer Bob Brown uneasy, so between meetings he marched from the meeting room across the field to the wooden goal-posts at the other end.

"He stopped at one of the goal-posts, got down in a three-point stance, put his right foot back for leverage, then put a forearm smash on the goalpost," ex-Raiders coach John Madden wrote. "The goalposts swayed, then toppled backward, the crossbar tipping down. The Boomer had knocked down a goal post. Without a word, he got up and strode back to his awed teammates. The Boomer had arrived. What a Boom."

Compare him to another young player: Mack Lewis, the utlimate gentle giant. To help him lose weight, his St. Louis Cardinals coaches made him eat at a table limited to spare portions of diet food.

"But the weight never seemed to come off him," Alex Karras recalled. "He still weighed four tons. So the coaches followed him, and they discovered 15 minutes after his meal he was at the frozen custard stand down the road from the training camp eating three pails of ice cream. He couldn't help himself. The coaches kicked him out. I'm not sure he minded much. He was the best-humored man there ever was. He didn't care if he was in football or not."

NO. 59

Allow on-site wagering.

Loan sharks are OK, too, as well as "muscle" to help expedite the gaming process.

NO. 60

A Kickoff return for a touchdown can't be called back if it's too darn exciting.

Don't go technical on us with this clipping crap.

NO. 61

Art Modell Kiss-Off Day in Cleveland.

Give him a civic-sponsored middle-finger farewell.

NO. 62

Quarterbacks allowed to keep hands under center's butt for appropriate time - but no longer.

Looks strange. Is strange.

NO. 63

Summer camp for Rotisserie League geeks. Adult supervision provided.

Thirty-year-old males should be interested in women, not fourth-string quarterbacks.

Fresh air could help change their lives.

NO. 64

No such thing as unnecessary roughness.

NO. 65

Articulate coaches

"I got indicted into the Florida Sports Hall of Fame. They gave me a standing observation." - Florida State coach Bill Peterson.

"I'm the football coach around here, and don't you remember it" ...Peterson.

"We're not attempting to circumcise the rules," Pittsburgh Steelers coach Bill Cowher.

NO. 64

NO. 66

A few years back, an Oklahoma State running back said he'd never heard of Barry Sanders, who won the Heisman Trophy for the school and then became the NFL's best running back.

This is disgraceful.

Football players should be able to converse intelligently about football history, which is why all players should be required to pass a liscensing exam. Sample questions, include:

Red Grange was called Red because he:

A. Was a Commie.

B. It was his name.

C. He got embarrassed a lot.

What does the acronym NCAA stand for:

A. National Center for Disease Control

B. United States of America

C. Olympic Training Center.

D. Delta Airlines

E. None of the above.

F. National Collegiate Athletic Association

G. Only E

Who doesn't belong on this list:

1. Bradshaw and Swann

2. Montana and Rice

3. Aikman and Irvin.

4. Bert and Ernie

Which man doesn't own an NFL team:

1. Art Modell

2. Pat Bowlen

3. Ringo Starr

4. Jerry Jones.

Mike Ditka was:

A. A tantrum-throwing tight end for the Chicago Bears.

B. A tantrum-throwing assistant coach for the Dallas Cowboys.

C. A tantrum-throwing head coach for the Chicago Bears.

D. A tantrum throwing head coach for the New Orleans Saints.

E. All of the above.

NO. 67

No back-up quarterbacks.

NO. 68

First-in, first-out substitution.

NO. 69

Prevent prevent defenses:

"It is designed to prevent the other team from beating you with a bomb, so that they may march down the field and beat you with a field goal."

- Tex Schramm

NO. 70

Like steeplechase, create ponds and barriers players must leap over.

NO. 71

Make it illegal to smoke hash marks.

NO. 72

Ban end-zone celebrations except for men who know how to dance.

These days, conspicuousness passes for distinction. On the other hand, if a guy's a good break dancer ...

NO. 73

Helmets aren't mandatory.

NO. 74

Emphasize football's aesthetic side.

"The greatest thing about being a football player is that you don't have to take a shower to go to work" - Jay Hilgenberg, Chicago Bears.

"Hey, it's no different from sweating." Denver Broncos guard Mark Schlereth, explaining why he urinates while playing.

NO. 73

NO. 75

Big Daddy Lipscomb Postage Stamp

Let us pay tribute to one of football's original pieces of work. This mountain of a man stood 6-foot-6, weighed 300 pounds and slugged it out in the trenches in the 1950s when the game was populated by "oversized coal miners and West Texas psychopaths," says Art Donovan, one of Lipscomb's Baltimore Colts teammates.

Lipscomb liked to drop on piles of players knee-first to cause maximum pain to the limbs and torsos of opponents. He also wrapped his hands and forearms in tape, transforming them into deadly clubs.

More than anything, Big Daddy was an indomitable party man.

"I'm a BB Man - booze and broads."

NO. 76

Passing gas along the line of scrimmage is not allowed. (This is a malodorous area to start with. Besides, a true sportsman doesn't break wind in public.)

NO. 77

Combine Army, Navy and Air Force Academy into Pentagon State.

Team slogan: "I Want You."

NO. 78

Players are not allowed to engrave their name in their hair.

NO. 79

A no-contact clause for Deion Sanders.

Don't dent his persona.

NO. 80

No Cheerleaders with lengthy rap sheets.

NO. 81

Coaches who advocate family values.

"There will be no fighting in bar-rooms, unless the head coach is pinned down, in which case he should be rescued."

– Jerry Glanville.

NO. 80

NO. 82

Players who advocate family values.

"I don't care if my mother is out on the field. I'm going to smack her and take her face off and then apologize after the game." – Syracuse linebacker Don Conley.

NO. 83

World League Hall of Fame.

NO. 82

NO. 84

Encourage goal-setting by players.

"I want to gain fifteen hundred or two thousand yards, whichever comes first." – George Rogers.

NO. 85

National playoffs to determine worst Division I team.

Flush 'em out.

NO. 86

Bring back Buddy Ball.

NO. 87

Brawling players must appear before Judge Wapner.

Mandatory sentencing.

NO. 88

Easier college entrance exams for football players.

Not all of 'em are potential scholars. Or potential students. So chill, Mr. Professor.

A few sample questions on the Iowa Hawkeye Test of Basic Skills for Gridders.

What language is spoken in Spain?

A. Spanish

B. None

How many teams compete in the Big 12?

A. 12

B. 0

C. 1

D. A couple hundred.

When was the War of 1812 Fought?

A. 1812

B. Last year.

C. The year before that.

What lies between North America and South America?

A. Central America

B. The North Pole

C. The South Pole.

What is England?

A. A web-site.

B. A board game

C. A country.

NO. 89

Macho coaches.

"He treats us like men. He lets us wear ear-rings." - University of Houston receiver Torrin Polk on Cougars coach John Jenkins.

NO. 90

Break-up them Bengals.

NO. 91

Encourage self-pride.

"We've got to find a way to win. I'm willing to start cheating," said New England tight end Marv Cook.

At the Pro Bowl, a woman asked Scott Adams if he was playing in the game. "No," he said, "I play for the Atlanta Falcons."

"I don't think there's going to be that many people writing books this year. We don't have that many people who can read and write." - Cornerback Mark Collins, comparing the New York Giants Super Bowl XXI and XXV championship teams.

NO. 92

600-pound weight limits.

Three-hundred-and-fifteen pound Washington Redskins guard Ray Brown sits in a barber's chair and it collapses.

Three-hundred-thirty-five pound Jets tackle James Brown hits a bump in the road while driving his truck and his seat collapses.

Three-hundred-and-forty pound Bengals defensive tackle Keith Rucker and four teammates sit down on five connected chairs at an airport - each anchored to a single steel support beam - and all five seats come crashing down.

A Minnesota Vikings guard has to be transported to a weigh-in station for livestock because he's just too much for the team scale.

NO. 92

Cleveland Browns offensive tackle Orlando Brown weighs 324 pounds and wears a size-64 suit coat.

A Miami high school boasts four linemen who weight close to 1300 combined pounds.

In the Wide, Wide World of Sports, no one is wider and freakier than America's corn (and-everything else) fed linemen, with the possible exception of Japanese Sumo wrestlers, who may not be Homo Sapiens.

Enact the Fat Cap.

Equatorial waistlines, blueberry torsos, and elephantine legs were not what football's founding fathers had in mind when they gathered a century ago in the Superdome.

"The coaches thought he would be all-pro. He turned out to be all-cafeteria." - Houston Oilers general manager Ladd Herzog after releasing 300-pound Angelo Fields.

"Now I look like a normal fat human being" - San Francisco 49ers offensive tackle Bubba Paris, describing his 340-pound frame after dropping 40 pounds.

NO. 93

Witness Protection plan for controversial sportswriters.

These guys have hearts like cash-registers. Nevertheless, they shouldn't be bull's-eyes for rampaging players. The history of scribe abuse is drenched in blood.

Mean Joe Greene spits in a reporter's face. Jim McMahon blows his nose on another. A Houston reporter gets in an acerbic exchange with Oilers quarterback Dan Pastorini, who pushes him through a half-open door leading to a practice field. They both land at the feet of Oilers coach Bum Phillips, who had been telling an interviewer on how well his team got along with the media.

NO. 93

NO. 94

Full-time bail bondsman for Dallas Cowboys.

Maybe two.

These dudes come from the wrong side of the white picket fence.

NO. 95

A union for capologists.

NO. 96

Encourage players to see the big picture.

In 1978 New England coach Chuck Fairbanks was suspended on the eve of the playoffs when owner Billy Sullivan discovered he would soon take the University of Colorado job.

"Does that mean there won't be a Christmas party at Fairbanks' house?" one player asked.

NO. 97

Cheerleaders must conceal tattoos.

NO. 98

Fine players who repeatedly refer to themselves in third person.

End megalomania in my, er, our, time...

NO. 99

On-field cell phones for quarterbacks.

Includes Caller-Id.

NO. 100

Simple game plans.

"Defensively, I think it's important to tackle," – Karl Mecklenburg before the Denver Broncos' Superbowl XXIV game against San Francisco.

NO. 99

NO. 101

Free beer for all at training camp.

Beer helps the bonding process, and football is all about bonding. In fact, tens of millions of Americans unite around the pigskin sport every fall. Which is why we call ourselves the United States of America.

Maybe we overdo it at times, but who cares. Everyone benefits. At Super Bowl I, the Los Angeles Coliseum was half-empty, tickets cost as little as $6, and the game opened like a yawn to a national television audience.

But more people watched the Super Bowl in 1970 than Neil Armstrong's first steps on the moon a few months before.

And we've been lost in space ever since. Take the Barrel Man, for example. In the 1980s he shot to fame as the Denver

Broncos' No. 1 booster by leading cheers clad in only a large barrel and a cowboy hat. Several years ago, the Barrel Man called it quits during a teary press conference.

But when the going gets tough, the Barrel Man gets barreling. He came back stronger than ever for Super Bowl XXXII, leading fans to the Promised Land, with a little help from John Elway and Co.

With these 101 suggestions, we're trying to help too. We believe we have everything figured out about this wonderful sport except for one thing:

How does the Barrel Man sit-down?

Clay Latimer is an award winning sports writer for *The Rocky Mountain News*, which he joined in 1982. He has covered college football, the NBA, skiing, golf, the Denver Nuggets and, since 1995, the Denver Broncos. He is a member of the National Sportscaster and Sportswriter Association and is a three time winner of the Colorado Sports Feature Story of the Year. Latimer is the author of *John Elway: Armed and Dangerous* the story of John Elway's career, including his Super Bowl XXXII triumph over the Green Bay Packers.

Other Addax Sports-Humor Books

Jockularity: The Sports Cartoons of Brad Kirkland - Volume 1
Applying the principle that nothing is so good that it can't be
laughed at, *Jockularity* offers a collection of sports cartoons
lampooning just about every facet of every sport. 144 pages.
Black and white illustrations throughout. Retail price $10.95.

**Mulligans 4 All! 101 Excuses, Alibis and Observations on
the Game of Golf by Chuck Carlson**
This humorous book offers 101 ways to make golf fun, fulfilling,
interesting and may even cut down on your use of words you
don't want your children saying. Hilarious cartoons highlight
the action. Hardcover, 144 pages. More than 35 black and
white illustrations. Retail price $9.95.

To order individual or bulk copies of
these books please contact.
Addax Publishing Group, Inc.
8643 Hauser Drive, Suite 235
Lenexa, KS 66215
1-800-598-5550